Canticle of Light and Dark

Paula Sayword

cover photo by the author, author photo by Karen Sims

Acknowledgement is made to the editors of the journals and anthologies in which the following poems, in earlier versions, first appeared: *Naugatuck River Review*: Fourth of July; *Sinister Wisdom*: Corinth, Vermont & Polly Unfound; *Cyclamens and Swords*: The Way Home; *The Zuni Mountain Poets-an Anthology*: Liturgy of the Hours; *Querencia—a Mini Anthology of Poems*: Book of Dreams

With much gratitude for all who helped with this manuscript, especially Ann McNelly's careful editing; Tim Amsden, Jack Carter North, and Susie Patlove for their generous and helpful comments. A thank you to Carol Potter for her expert guidance, the Friday Morning Seminar poets for their ongoing support, Didi Firman for her friendship, and always my deep appreciation to Karen for believing in me. A special thanks to my departed friend, Jean Laino, whose financial gift made this publication possible.

Published by the Synthesis Center Press
Amherst, Massachusetts

ISBN 978-0-99095900-7
Library of Congress Control Number: 2014955998

Technical editor: Ted Slawski
Set in Goudy Oldstyle & Goudy Handtooled typefaces

For my grandchildren,
Dayne and Emme
and always for Ashley

Contents

IV

V

Book of Dreams

The day stretches beneath a cold indifferent sky
and a certain sorrow rises, a peculiar forgotten prayer

that no longer sings but catches in the throat
like memory or the need for salvation.

And sometimes there comes a terrible beauty
or a mouthful of sin, a small meanness,

if not here, then somewhere else and we ask ourselves
what comes stumbling as the night gathers?

Who walks the road with a twisted cane and a shuffle?
What hides on the other side of our long slow dying?

There are stories old and thick with desire.
They sleep in a book we forget to open,

even though the book calls out our names
and on each page is another name for god.

If we opened the book, would we dream ourselves home,
trusting the answers are found inside the words?

Or would we wonder how the river of all we thought
we knew rests silent, like a bed of stones?

I

Middle Street

On the map, a street,
a short cross-through street,
with only one house,
600 square feet,
a bungalow,
built in 1940
next to a vacant lot with
an old cherry tree.
The house smells of salt and tears,
someone left behind.
The house is not for sale.
It is crooked, beaten
and a little out of breath.
It has no basement,
a porch full of forgotten things,
a bedroom facing Long Island Sound
where once during a hurricane
window glass shattered all over
my parent's bed.
Years ago I drew a circle
on this dirt road,
a circle for a game of marbles,
a circle for memory
and constellations in the sky.
The circle is still inside me,
so too the smell of mud flats,
the whistle of a calliope.
On the map, a middle street.
I can place my finger on it,
feel the child shift inside,
the one left behind.

February, 1951

A little girl sits at a strange kitchen table
trying to eat a bowl of Cream of Wheat.

She struggles to not fidget but her braids are too loose,
her favorite shoes left behind.

Uncle Walter smiles as if he knows a secret.
Aunt Genie talks so loud it makes the girl's teeth hurt.

The child remembers the ice-storm morning,
her father pouring hot water on car door handles,

rushing to get her mother to the hospital, the baby coming.
Trees on fire, frozen sunlight trapped in the crystals.

She remembers her baby brother brought home and
her grandmother dying, and all she can hear is her mother's

weeping behind the closed bedroom door,
her father's silence, the baby crying all the time.

She remembers her own face in the train window,
her name pinned to a red plaid jacket,

going somewhere all alone with the darkness outside,
the new baby and her parents at home without her.

Now she sits, her Uncle still smiling and her Aunt
telling her "eat-up before it gets cold." The cereal feels

lumpy, lonely in her mouth, and, gagging she tries not to cry.
Steam like thin wool shrouds the windows.

Fourth of July
for bob

I don't suppose you remember that time.
You were five or so. I must have been ten.
We had ridden in the rear of the Pontiac,
upholstery itchy on our bare legs.
Dad driving, smoking his Camels.
Mom humming *Stormy Weather*,
smiling her sad smile, her voice
the sound of faint morning rain.

We had driven to some broken down
road side stand in another state,
where an old man and woman
sold ice cold soda and fireworks,
birch beer, Coca-Cola,
cherry bombs, rockets and sparklers.

Restless, we chased across the dirt road
into a wide high meadow,
your voice behind me, a laughing bell.
Just before dusk thought of itself,
the summer sun fell flushed and ruddy,
into the tall grass, its glow caught
in clots of foam. "Snake spit" we called it.

Fireflies appeared as we were leaving,
shimmered like small galaxies
drifting through our childhood.
You whined, wanted to light the sparklers,
settled for sucking your thumb.
Dad turned on the radio, switched
the knob till he found Jimmy Dorsey
playing *So Rare*. You fell asleep and our
parents spoke quietly, as if I were not there.

Charlie

The ice cream man drove his truck
through a humid August dusk, the air
smelling of mowed lawns, hot dogs on the grill.
After dinner his bell called to them,
children who begged quarters from tired fathers
then ran laughing, shoving to be first in line.

He had the bluest eyes, a quick smile,
a voice soft like the scent of lemons,
uniform pressed white, crisp,
name stitched above the left pocket.
Charlie, it said. He had been there all summer.

She was the last one at the window,
the others had scattered, gone home
before dark like so many blackbirds,
their laughter fading as he asked
if she wanted to see inside the truck,
open the metal lids of his ice-cold boxes.

When he lifted her up and pulled her close
his hand suddenly inside her red shorts,
she didn't know what was happening.
His voice still soft, blue eyes smiling,
breath hot against her neck.

She ran home inside the collapsing dark,
her ears filled with nothing
but the hard slap of sneakers on pavement.
A toasted almond ice cream melting in her hand,
bell fading far in the distance.

Remembering Grand Manan Island, 1971

Stephen walked the beach lost inside his own emptiness.
He thought if he could retrieve pieces of ruined dreams,
as if they were stones and shells within his reach,
it might have made a difference.
But he knew nothing would ever be the same,
not since breathing the stifling air
in that god forsaken country.
It was in him still, trapped, hot and heavy,
choking him like blood, like mud.
His wife was not the woman he remembered,
his newborn son unfamiliar, crying day and night.
He wanted to get high, stay high on the Thai stick
he smuggled back to the States, then nothing
would matter. Nothing would matter at all.

I sat on the white porch,
my breath coming softly into a flute.
Its sound was sad as the falling afternoon light,
the color of everything I saw.
There had once been a flame burning in my body,
now I felt no light was left.
I wondered why the wind blew wide
through my belly as if I were not there,
as if I were someone even I didn't know.
From the porch high on the bluff I watched
him at the water's edge, a stranger now.
He was walking away into the dying sun.
Our baby was quiet, finally asleep,
dreaming of his origins, beginning to forget.

The Way Home

A curtain of snow closes in, first the far hills,
then closer, the valley gone, trees blotted out,
the sky pulls down fast and hard and a great flock
of pinon jays is the only blue.

One Sunday afternoon people spoke of the way home
as if anyone knew the way through the oil canvas,
acrylic paintings hanging on the wall or
the naked coyote skull bright with nail polish,

to enter the smell of crimson paint and golden wax,
bones of the dead, the burnt fur of forgetting,
the hiss and cluck of our tongues as they run
over our teeth, our unspoken needs.

Is home where plates of food sit waiting,
steaming on a wooden table, laid out with
careful hands, a little girl humming softly
in the doorway of the kitchen or is it in

blood on our knees as we crawl up
the long stone steps to the empty stars
where god and mary and all the angels
hide behind a crazed light promising forever.

Is home what we imagine we remember
being held close to a beating heart,
our cheeks flushed hot with sweat,
blue rim of breast milk on our eager lips,

or is it the desire and delight as a lover stirs
between our legs, singing us beyond all the
words we ever knew, where panting and sated
we beg for something close to mercy.

Are the directions home slipped in a corner
of an old map where our handwriting is illegible
yet we understand its meaning, the colors staining
our fingers with a faith we thought we'd lost?

The pinon jays move off, treetop to treetop
and still the snow comes in, thick with silence,
a vast smudge of gray, smoky and dense,
layered over what is left of our lives.

Return

Far off thunder,
air soaked with moisture
as if breathing underwater
were an easy thing to do
and I try to remember
what thirsty space sounded like.
The green is dense,
tender, forgiving,
grass beads wet,
cool under bare feet,
unseen tree frogs trilling
into late afternoon.
I feel my voice everywhere,
hear it as I watch
fog devour the hills I love.
Nothing obvious
as I stand slightly bent,
my empty hands
holding an echo,
a dry whisper
of something I cannot call back.

II

Satchel of Psalms

In the bony branches of a lilac bush,
mourning doves hunch like praying monks,
their russet-blue robes riffled against the cold.

They remind her of another winter, of stillness
and lost voices, of a time long ago when she

crossed a wilderness with a satchel of psalms.
The psalms sang to her as she wandered a forest burdened
by snow, crystals sifting down, a vague shimmer

of faith as she trudged on alone through slumbering trees,
no compass, no map to mark the way home.

Her breath huffed in the bitter air, grew brittle,
sparkled as night fell and the stars came cold,
shaking in a black net of sky. An owl hooted,

a lonely sound just beneath rising wind, until
far off another answered from the moonless dark.

She pulled a wool cloak closer to her face.
It smelled faintly of frankincense and candle wax,
offered her refuge from the icy slivered air.

The crucifix was far behind her now, so too penance
 and the saints with their sad, luminous eyes.

She followed a single deer track in the snow,
could see a distant light in the window of her cabin.
Everything safe and sheltered, the secretive owls

watching and crying into the night-noise of the forest.
Psalms singing softly. Doves hushed with sleep.

Thirst

She used to think of God when the earth turned toward the
gathering light of morning, meeting the sun for another day
but not now, not for many years. There had been Mass every
morning, thin white wafer, dry body of Christ on her tongue
and a longing, always a longing bound to the sense she could
be love in the world, could believe in anything, but not now.
She wonders if she is inside or outside life's meaning.
The house of herself empty. The joy she hungers for,
still elusive, its wings barely flutter against her cheek.
No word she speaks, no word she writes, no word she hears
can fill the longing that holds her like an old lover.

On the side of the road two dogs gnaw on a deer carcass.
The sky is an odd shade of blue and somewhere in the wind
she hears the wails of war, moans of hungry children.
She doubts there is magic in the bottom of her glass,
enlightenment in an eye of the moon or the cold stars.
She wants to believe in something the way she used to,
faith or grace or the idea of God, but she can't seem to
summon any meaning home. Far away a woman draws
a blanket over the limp body of a child. There is blood
in the dust, bombs bursting and a low moan in the orchard.
A red bird sings in the ragged branches.

Now That You're Gone
for l.t.

You gave away pieces of a younger life,
turquoise belt buckle, collection of arrow heads,
old shears for working leather.
You had no use for them,
time whittled down to reading your life away,
in a one room apartment,
sipping watered-down whiskey all day.
Remembering.
You told stories of growing up in the Valley.
Mama dead when you were twelve,
daddy gone off, lost to drink and loneliness,
raising yourself, five siblings.
You washed laundry till your knuckles bled,
drove the buckboard to town for suppers,
square dancing at the Grange Hall.
Then there was Helen.
You were two women together more than thirty years,
banty-hens scratching in the yard, goats to milk,
cages filled with the rabbits you bred and sold.
Did desire singe your body
as you fastened your lives around each other,
chaste and alone in your beds at night,
dreaming of something you had no language for?
I imagine you, elbows on your knees,
dungarees turned up at the ankles,
smoking a hand-rolled cigarette by the wood cook stove,
as Helen read her poems to you by kerosene light.
Death took her first, lungs lost to cancer
and her daughter denied you those last days
as Helen lay dying, so that grief always held you
silent and hard like flint or an unyielding sky.
You stayed on alone until that long last winter,
body gone frail, cabin too cold.

You would have died there if they hadn't forced you
to sell the animals you loved, leave the Amherst woods
and come to this small apartment on the fifth floor.
Now you sit day after day in an old soft chair,
facing a black and white photograph of Helen
smiling back at you. You drink your whiskey,
read western novels and tell me stories of your life.

Polly Unfound

All those years ago I loved her
even though I knew I should not.
She had a husband, so did I,
both of them off in the sweat and death of a jungle
far away from the hills of Vermont.

All summer we worked together.
At night we drank bottles of Molson Ale,
smoked cigarettes, listened to the dark slosh
of Lake Champlain against the shore,
sometimes talking until the sky burned awake.

There were no words for what I felt when she
leaned in close, the smell of her, incense and soap,
no language for what stirred in my belly.
I never spoke of it to her. I was married.
So was she. They were coming home.

My husband returned with his burden of war,
his starving heart, taking me away from her.
On the drive south I cried, afraid I might die
with the choke and snot of it and that first night lying
beneath him, a desperate loneliness swelled inside me.

Years later language blossomed, fell from my tongue
like a rich spice and I stood alone holding
a baptism of words in my open hands.
I told her I was in love with a woman,
had left my marriage. She never spoke to me again.

Provincetown Remembered

She was walking crowded
Commercial Street on a July afternoon,
wearing cut-off corduroy jeans,
tank top, lace-up work boots,
skin tanned to perfection.
She had nowhere to go, no one to be.
It was before she cut her hair,
still hand rolled her cigarettes,
tough dyke who slept with all her friends.
The street was full of tourists,
moms and dads, kids sauntering behind,
eating ice cream, slices of pizza,
watching half-dressed gay boys
kissing at the corner,
drag queens on roller skates
flying down toward the wharf.
The fishing boats were coming in
with their daily catch of blues and sea bass,
flounder and lobster.
Wind blew in off the Bay,
rigging creaked and clanked,
competing with the voices of men hollering
as they off-loaded their fish,
joking about beer and sex,
the fireworks later that night.
She sat on a bench,
squinted into the sea light,
closed her eyes
and listened to the clanking, the voices,
the boats rubbing against the dock.
Music started playing in a bar up the beach
and she could just make out
a disco beat on the wind,
knew after the fireworks were finished

she would go down the alley to that bar,
drink a few beers,
dance with strange and beautiful women
to the music of Donna Summer,
get hot and sweaty
and stand out on the deck
under a cool mesh of stars,
the tide coming in salty and brave,
the tide coming in.

Let Her Ride

It's 7 a.m. and Jane is drinking her second cup of coffee alone, the way she does every morning but this morning as the sky turns from gray to a vacant blue all she can think about is getting in her car, lighting a cigarette she hasn't smoked in 30 years and driving fast, as fast as she can, blaring old CD's like *Abbey Road*, *Disraeli Gears* or maybe *Beggars Banquet*, so she could sing along with "Sympathy for the Devil" as loud as she wants, with nobody to hear and nobody to care that she is smoking again, driving too fast and still wondering who killed the Kennedys. Maybe if she can get the car going fast enough she might dissolve into the past, explode through some time barrier to cruise along the Mother Road of Route 66, before I-40 and the litter of McDonalds, Love Truck Stops and Walmarts. Jane wants to drive past motor courts, grocery stores that have gas pumps out front with flying red horses painted on them and diners with names like Roy's Place or Ruby's Café, where a piece of coconut cream pie costs thirty-five cents and coffee a dime. She craves a route across the lonely heartland and high plains of America, before her face had lines etched around her eyes and her mouth had not yet become her mother's mouth, before her husband lost his mind patrolling the Mekong River after his buddy's guts splattered all over his lap. And she wishes she could fall asleep at night and not worry how dying will take her hand and lead her some place she might not want to go. But it's only 7 am and Jane has to get dressed to go to a job she has hated for years, relieved it is nearly time to retire, but afraid she'll retire to an empty room of white walls with nothing to do but dream day after day of driving way too fast, blaring The Rolling Stones, careening down some flat lonesome road.

When We Were Golden

When we were young
and our children were golden,
I handed you a book of poems.
I handed you my heart.
In the soft green of spring
we lay in bed under
an open window,
listening to the faint flute
of a thrush in the trees.
Our bodies singing.

That summer the children swam
naked in a north woods lake,
laughter in their throats,
wild blueberry stains on their fingers.
Free in the summer dark.
At night our golden puppy waited
on the cabin porch while we camped
in the island's lean-to,
fell asleep to the yodel of loons.
Time was liquid, perfect, sweet.

Tenderness lost.
Laughter caught on a thorn.
The children, thick as blackflies
fought and whined, your parents hated me,
hated who we were together.
We lost the road map.
The needle on the compass
could fix in no direction.
The poetry we had been
struggled to find life on the page.

All winter you brooded in that long woolen coat.
I tried to save us. I wanted to be cruel,
wanted to hate you, punish myself.
Drove the car with no heat into the January cold,
tree limbs snapped,
birds froze, fell from brittle branches.
The sky cracked, broke inside my chest.
You said you loved me,
oh, you always loved me,
but you left over and over again.

Driving Home 6:30 a.m., August, 1984
for karen

Over back country roads
the summer morning swells into dawn,
awakens like my heart beating inside
its confine of bone and dread.
How to risk love again as I fall
into the clear sky of you.

Last night separateness dissolved
like breath against skin
your mouth, hands, heart loved me
until every cell exploded into light.

You gathered me in your arms,
murmuring a sound so tender I thought
I would weep with the joy and grief of it.
A surrender, a trust in possibility,
the way flowers open at daybreak with
the promises of nothing and everything.

Her Last Winter

My mother used to fall asleep on the couch
after dinner each night,
head sinking towards her chest,
snapping back with a snore.
Sadness and secrets trapped inside,
loneliness shuddering through her even at rest.
There were no words for the regrets
she clutched like tarnished coins
in the palm of her hand,
or the simple things she denied herself—
wine colored scarf for her arthritic neck,
a cat to keep her warm through winter,
bunch of yellow flowers on the kitchen table.
My mother waited for the sky to turn blue,
waited for life to happen,
waited to split out of her skin.
Every day she would drive to the beach,
pull her collar up, hold it closed tight
against her neck with hands bare and cold
in the wind off the Sound.
Laughing gulls shouted overhead.
Least sandpipers skittered around the sea ice.
Waves green and silver rolled, hummed over the sand.

What Matters

I lie in bed, do not hear
the wind rattle windows,
thrash the pinon trees.
Outside the house nothing matters.
I wonder
if this is what dying might be like,
the breaking away of matter,
the letting go of what the day is doing.
I am far inside
caught under throbbing skin.
My *eyes feel sick*, I say
and so I close them,
stay inside.
It does not matter that clouds shift
through a sky of perfect blue.
I dream and wake,
make words for a poem,
wake and dream
of oxeye daisies in a mason jar,
the white ones with pinwheel petals,
yellow heart,
three blue flag iris for company,
perhaps a tiny yellow spider inside.

Corinth, Vermont
for carol

It was summer, full summer,
swollen with smells of ripening corn,
sweet fern and blackberries in the sun,
rot of leaves in the woods.
The sky had been cloudless all day,
wind soft against our skin,
two women past sixty, lovers long ago,
now friends across a weave of time.
There were poems still, geography of aging,
grandchildren, another new lover for you,
me with a long time partner,
and as we climbed the dirt path up a wide green hill,
our faces told all the stories
we may not have uttered,
although no one heard what we said,
no one saw us sitting on the top of that hill
looking out on forever with mountains
far away under a blue hymn of sky.
Afterward, as I drove the road making turns
past the poverty of rusted mobile homes,
old houses leaning in on themselves
and small farms with signs offering
fresh eggs for three dollars a dozen,
a reddened sun was falling behind the Vermont hills.
Up ahead lay the highway winding south,
with miles to drive before I reached home
and I remembered the sound of a thrush
while we had eaten dinner outside,
the sound coming from somewhere off in the woods,
how each note was a kind of memory strung together.
Time dropping behind, headlights coming on.

Hymn of Lost Time

Sister Cyprian walks through a winter garden,
hem of her habit crusted with snow.

She remembers plants in bloom then harvest,
how birds came to the bath in summer,

and flowers of cobalt and crimson graced the walk,
always a scent of crushed herbs under her heavy shoes.

All barren now but for brittle sprigs of rosemary pushing
through snow at the foot of a stone St. Francis.

The sky is gray and thick, scattered flurries obscure
her vision as she passes through the dormant orchard.

She wanders through the cemetery. So many gone,
asleep under earth and snow in simple pine boxes.

She has loved her sisters well these past sixty years,
perhaps too much, she thinks, as she approaches the

graves of those she remembers, of one she wanted
to touch but never dared, never whispered the desire.

She knows everything passes, feels her own frailty
as she slowly kneels before Jesus dying on the cross.

For a moment she wonders if any of it was true—sin
and sacrifice, obedience, canons of the Church—but

what matters now is the rustling sound of cloth
as they settle in their pews, the voices of her sisters

praying softly in the hushed light of their wooden chapel,
breaking bread together in the quiet refectory.

The old nun rises, brushes snow from her skirt,
adjusts the scapula and pulls a woolen shawl tighter.

So much time spent walking these convent grounds,
so much time wandering inside all the silence.

III

Liturgy of the Hours*

I   Lauds

A woman steps outside, fastens a clasp on her cloak, thinks
about the day in front of her, the week, time's passage

opening wide, unfurling too fast, the way spring shudders,
everything lush all at once, close, drunk on itself.

If only the years had not suddenly stumbled away, her
children past middle age, her face a story the lines tell.

She sees a shroud of mist and fog, bobolinks sinking into
wet grass, taking their songs into the quivering green.

Cool drizzle holds her and together they walk backward
through other springs, through vibration beneath the air.

She believes it is vespers on the planet, dusk in the hearts
of its creatures. She can hear it in the breath of birds,

smell it on the wind, sense it in the marrow of her
sorrowful bones. She thinks of the earth as blue animal,

gut-shot and slowly bleeding out. It raises and shakes its
wounded self. Huffs, thrashes in pain. Trees fall. Waters

rise. Bedrock trembles. She fears for her grandchildren, for
what all children will inherit, the end of songbirds, glaciers

and the singing wind. She hears greed and religion crying
out in supplication: *money, money, jesus, mary and joseph,*

*money and allah, jehova and god, god why hath thou
forsaken us?* She hears all the saints and martyrs crying

out with weeping hands and flayed flesh, virgins in heaven,
nuns in the poor house, piles of coins on the boardroom

floor. She imagines the soft chime of a bell, remembers,
stops to smooth the hem of her cloak. She gets down on

her knees to light a candle at the base of an old statue, her
loneliness a weight of stones.

Where is the silky sun, she wonders? The magic flute
player and ruby colored dragonflies, wise abuela* of a

peach-blossomed valley? Where are they before it is
too late, before she hears the last bird cry out from

the fallen forest and the bones of the dead clattering
deep in the quivering green grass?

II   Vespers to Prime

The blue animal gasps. Great plumes of fire lick the air,
suck blue out of the sky. The sun, blood red in daylight.

There is a great weeping of wind. Far away she smells a
burnt odor of caramel and vanilla as trees of Ponderosa

pine catch, burst with fire. She mutters prayers as she steps
along the path, sensing her face sting with a drift of cinders

raining dark in the distant west. Dusk has come with half-
light and shadow. She hears a bell sound somber.

A breeze unexpectedly slips in from the north. She pulls
her threadbare cloak tighter, moves off the path and allows

the forest to take her in, the way it hides owl and fox, a
spotted fawn. She walks long. She will sleep here she

thinks, make of the night a canticle she can chant as
darkness settles. All night she breathes in the lonely stars,

dreams of rain dances in the west, hears a jingle of ankle
bells and the howling sky. Before dawn a heavy mist lays

itself down and the leaves sip slowly. Her cloak is wet.
She shakes off sleep and emerges half wild from the woods.

There are seeds, twigs in her long hair. A stench of rot in
the leaf and duff. She is not sure where she is, afraid for a

moment that she might drown, the green around her
drenched and deep. She gulps for air. A hermit thrush

sings praises to the morning and through the fog she hears
a flute or think she does, follows its call to the worn path.

She has lived alone too long. She hears things. She sees
what is not there, feels the blue animal's pain in her belly,

knows fires still rage far away, the early light soaked with
thick dry smoke. Mule deer and wolves exhausted from

running all night. She fingers the prayer beads in her
pocket. Her lips move without sound as she returns to

her gardens. In the doorway of her cabin, she pauses and
looks back on where she has been. But she sees nothing.

The mist hangs heavy, moist, still. She wonders if during
the long night someone else has come to sleep inside her.

In the kitchen she takes off her cloak, puts a kettle on to
boil, hums to herself, sifts yeast into a wooden bowl.

III   Terce to Sext

The blue animal pants with pain, throws its head back,
yowls. The wind is fierce, rattles the shutters of her cabin.

Fog has finally lifted. The air is clean and high, sky a color
blue she has not seen in a long time. It offers a kind of

baptism, she thinks. Color deep as any water she has ever
seen, but the battering turn of wind forces her back inside.

She closes the windows against thundering air, the day
different than the one she emerged from just hours ago.

On the rear of the wood stove dough is rising in a dark red
bowl. The smell of yeast and honey settle in the kitchen.

She sits at the table with a stale crust of bread, soft goat
cheese, tender and bitter greens on a chipped plate.

The cabin trembles in a heave of wind, the gray cat
startles, disappears into another room. The chimes outside

her door clang, slam against the wall. What is to become
of us, she wonders, opening the book of psalms she has

written herself. The cover is deep brown leather, its pages
hand sewn, paper vellum-like, supple, her handwriting,

sure and true. She wrote it a long time ago in another
place, at an older table, the casita floor, a cool red earth

under her naked feet. She begins to read aloud:
Oh beloved Earth turn your face to me…but the shutters

smash and knock, a painting of a sleeping woman and a
yellow dog in a field of blueberries falls to the floor, the

glass shattering. A gust growls down the chimney, rattles
the lid on the stove, the entire cabin seems to quake.

Outside, the trees wail and thrash, beat against the sky.
She closes her book, her whole body is shaking.

This is not a wind of the East, she thinks, getting up
to collect broken glass. It is a wind of the West,

unsettled, seeking and lost, like the voice still caught
inside her, the one that weeps towards the sun at noon,

the one who knows and cannot say, the one who says and
cannot know. The one always lost.

IV   None

By mid-afternoon the wind has cried itself out and gone off
to sleep somewhere else. Outside her cabin the air is

weightless as a ghost. Her garden is in ruins, plants
shredded, bean and tomato poles snapped, fruit bruised and

bleeding into the soil. She will save what can be saved,
leave the rest to feed the dirt. No use fretting over what

cannot be salvaged. She knows the days are too short for
that kind of regret. Suddenly she feels an unutterable

hunger deep in her belly and knows she must leave this
place that has been her home for so long. She works for

hours in her garden, scrabbling among its stalks and leaves,
collects what vegetables she can into a woven basket

and returns to the cabin where the smell of fresh baked
bread lingers in the air. How will she go, she wonders?

How much money has she saved from selling eggs
and psalms, wild honey and the harvest from her garden?

She slices a slab of bread, slathers it with apple butter,
tastes her labor and smiles. Gray cat stretches on the

windowsill and yawns. How can she abandon him? He has
been with her so long. The flock of chickens will go feral,

roost low in the trees, lay their eggs for the fox to eat. She
has no worry for them or any of her possessions, but

how she will care for herself? She is no longer a young
woman, not the woman who left her life and children

once before. She lived on the edge of the desert then,
writing her cantos and verse, tending a herd of goats on

the rocky hillside, playing a flute with the liturgy of the
hours. It is where she first heard the blue animal sigh.

No, she is not that woman and yet she is. *We are always
who we were*, she says aloud, dumping out a glass jar

stuffed with coins, paper money. She counts and thinks.
She cannot remember why she left the West, wonders if

the Refuge is still there with the iron bell tolling high in
the tower, beckoning all who can hear to come and dream.

She hears it now coming from within. It shifts in her belly
and the sound is hypnotic. What voice, what hunger is this

that speaks? Did she lose her mind in the forest?
How can she leave this cabin she built with her own

hands? Or the sheltering green of the woods and the skies
with heavy pewter clouds that soften all edges? How can

she leave to return to a geography of blue-drenched sky
and bony rock, valley outside of time where someone

might remember her name? She smooth's out the
currency, stacks the coins; knows she has enough for a

a bus or a train. She gave up her car long ago. Yes, it must
be the train, she thinks, to rumble her west, carry her tired

body across a landscape she has not seen in thirty years,
through strange cities and the junk yards of democracy.

V   Vespers to Matins

The woman boards the train in late afternoon. There is a
luminous shimmer in the trees on the far side of the tracks.

It is lovely she thinks, this dying light. Her knees feel stiff
as she ascends the metal steps and catching her foot on

the hem of her skirt, she falters for a moment, the strap of
her knapsack slipping. She feels suddenly old.

There is no one to see her off. No one she has said
goodbye to. The conductor nods and takes the cat box

from her arms. It seems so heavy. She rests by the wide
windows that will open onto the nation as it rushes past,

the country she so loves, her lost America. The cat is at
her feet, knapsack next to her. She folds her cloak,

arranges it behind her head. A whistle blows, the train
lurches, halts, starts again, slowly pulls out of the station.

She knows she will never return to her cabin of wood and
stone. She will not take another journey. This will be her

last passage and will bring her back to the beginning, or
what she thinks of as the beginning. She looks down at

her hands. They seem unexpectedly fragile, blue-veined
and thin. They flutter for a moment, a flock of lost birds.

She wonders if they are someone else's hands. She reaches
down, touches her cat through the holes in the box.

She has bread and cheese, fried chicken wrapped in white
cloth, apples, and walnuts from her orchard. She eats,

shares her meal with gray cat and feels her life fall away
with the fading miles. The train settles into its rhythm,

a rocking rumble as she thinks about the leaf-smoke of
time, of departure and forgiveness and what she has left

behind, without a word to anyone, pulled by something
inexplicable, drawn by wind and a murmur from the

blue animal. There will be no pardon for us, she thinks as
dusk broadens toward night. She watches the country

diminish into darkness. Cities and desolation, families
camped in forests of broken trees, abandoned farmhouses,

the flicker of far off lights, then a long rolling into the
beyond. Stars spark in the flat distance of the sky. Her

heart is heavy and her bones ache. She reaches for the cat,
touches him softly and feels tears sting her eyes.

What have we done to ourselves? She pulls her cloak down
against a chill. The day collapses into midnight as she

rocks through a lingering emptiness, fingers the beads.
Inhales a faint scent of the blue animal and closes her eyes.

VI   After the Hours

When, at last, she arrives at the Refuge, old abuela
embraces her, whispers her name, a name she has not

heard in many years. Had she forgotten who she was?
They give her a room at the end of the plaza. Her old

adobe casita has fallen in with age and lays as a pile of
bricks down by the singing creek. This room is sparse but

spacious with windows opening to mountains the color of
smudged purple. They breathe against the distant sky,

their sloping face changing with the passing hours. From
the corner window she can see the stable and a corral, four

horses half asleep under a massive cottonwood. They lean
against each other, longtime companions, swishing flies,

dreaming the secret dream of horses. A boy brings her a
plate of sweet melon slices, cold lamb with newly-made

tortillas. The plate rests on the same wooden table where
she had written her psalms years ago. The woman eats a

little melon but her fatigue is overwhelming and she lays
down on the bed. It is soft under a quilt of faded colors

backed with wool. Gray cat stretches out next to her. She
has seen more ruin across the middle of America than she

could have imagined. How many devastated lives had she
passed? How much despair? Here at least she is no longer

alone with her knowledge of blue animal's pain. No one
here has forgotten. She hears the ancient windmill with

its three broken teeth catch a current of air to clank and
creak. Its sound soothes her. She feels as if everything

around her has waited with a great patience: the silent
rocks, the humming creek, the peach-blossomed valley,

wise abuela with her milky-blind eyes. How much longer
will time last, she wonders? Who will she be, now that she

remembers her own name? A raven lands on the window
sill, tilts its head and peers at her through the glass.

Can she really see a lift of sun in its dark eyes, a shimmer of
the cosmos in its black silken feathers? It taps the pane

two times, flaps its wings and suddenly disappears. The sky is an empty, dry blue. She is inside stillness.

She reaches out, strokes the sleeping cat. She knows there is not much time, but what there is, is all she has.

Flute music rises up from the dusty plaza and the sound of a bell ringing once in the tower. Only once.

She finally closes her eyes to feel a dream resting there. The wounded blue animal slowly comes to her,

a soft-footed sister, and the woman takes her in like a lover, filling them both with the slightest quiver of healing.

Her lips mumble a wordless chant. It is a beginning she thinks, falling asleep. A beginning.

*Notes: The Liturgy of the Hours are daily prayers within Christian Monasticism.

Lauds: Morning prayers at sunrise
None: Mid-afternoon
Prime: Early morning
Vespers: Evening
Terce: Midmorning
Compline: Night
Sext: Midday
Matins: Midnight

abuela: grandmother

IV

The Grandson

After a long day's hike through slot canyons, over red
slick-rock, a young man watches light slip towards slumber

in a western sky. He settles on a stone shelf, takes a
clementine from his pack and remembers how his

grandmother always brought him this fruit, a small sweet orange
she said came from faraway places like Morocco and Spain.

He remembers a lullaby she crooned to him until he was
too big for her arms to hold, some lullaby that made him

feel both sad and safe. He was the one she took on walks
through the shadowed woods, across bright fields of grass,

or out into the sapphire night where she spoke
to him about things he did not yet understand.

She would go away for a long time and he'd miss her, forget
her. But she always returned, her face growing more

creased with what he now knows was the luminous light
of the high desert. He is a man now, his grandmother

dead for more years than he knew her and now the past
seems to him like an orchard of things lost.

The stream where they tossed sticks and threw rocks
during humid summers is a dried-up trickle. Most of his

childhood forest is slashed to bramble and weeds and
nothing is as green as it used to be. He has left home in the

dwindling forests of the East to trek across a geography of
rock and sky, carrying the old back-pack she passed to him,

with words tucked in its pockets, shards of pottery and
juniper berries, sage dry as dust in the seams. He keeps

them, listens carefully as they murmur one to the
other, telling stories, holding counsel, reminding him to

walk the earth with quiet feet. Tonight he watches light
slip towards slumber in a western sky.

Darkness presses in, soundless. The rock face he leans
against has saved the warmth of the day inside itself.

He eats his clementine, some bread and cheese, pours two
fingers of bourbon into a tin cup from his grandmother's flask.

He is tired and welcomes the coming galaxy of night.
The young man thinks he hears her voice as a whisper in

the faint dry wind and for a moment he misses the forest of
his childhood. He unrolls his sleeping bag, sips his spirits.

The first stars flicker and he wonders on their ancient
passage. He considers making a small fire but

the stars will be brilliant if he lets the darkness have its
way. The night will be long.

Dove Creek

in memory of basil romero

Back when he was a younger man
he would pile the three dogs into his pickup
and drive north four hours to a small town
on a plateau of the Great Sage Plains.
He had come to buy dried Anasazi
and pinto beans in twenty-pound burlap sacks.

He loved the smell of that coarse cloth,
the heft of the beans in his arms,
enjoyed talking to the man in the general store
about the War before his War.
They would stand outside smoking cigarettes
in the leaning Colorado light,
looking off to the San Juan Mountains.

On his way home, he would stop
to visit the Ute elder at the trading post.
They would speak of their old ways,
Ute and Apache, of sorrow and things lost.

All these years later, uranium has ravaged
his lungs and he is too frail to drive.
He falls, can't remember, rages.
The old Ute is dead.

The grocery store is lopsided, abandoned.
On either side of the door, faded red letters—
Beans on one side, *Frijoles* on the other.
No one is around except a scrawny donkey
nudging hay on the ground near a broken fence.
The sky is gray with spits of snow
and we are just passing through.

The Memorial
for george

His brother was dead
and for hours the family drove
through the desert south of Tucson.
They had gray, gritty ashes to scatter
but no one could find his favorite place,
the site where he pitched
his tent to camp,
drinking cups of fiery whiskey,
smoking cigarette after cigarette,
forgetting to eat,
growing thin like the wind he
never saw
but felt blow through his bones.
As the day was ending
they came upon a wash near a
shelter of naked-branched cottonwoods.
It was a good place,
so they left their cars, said some
words and finally let him go.
In the January dusk
a flock of white-winged doves flew in,
settled at the lip of the wash
to drink what light
was still held in the water.
Someone whispered "listen"
and somewhere an owl hooted
once, twice
and was silent.

Rumors

In memory of k.u.

They said Kenny left in the middle of a red windstorm,
his broken-down van swaying along I-40.
An old lover had been beaten in the men's room
of the Lubbock bus station and needed to be rescued.
He always needed to be rescued,
wild birds in his back pockets,
wild birds in his boots, flapping and moaning,
flying off, chaos wherever he went.
But Kenny loved the man with the wild birds,
deserted everything for him, his home,
even his dogs, who finally wandered off
dragging their broken hearts up into the hills.
Kenny left and never came back.

Was he pulled by the memory of his restless roots,
carnival tents up, snake oil under colored lights,
a ride on the Ferris-wheel for three tickets?

One time I sat by a fire with him,
looking up at stars swarming thick in a black sky.
He told me his heart was not whole,
that cells were dying in the marrow of his bones.
Then he left the party, walked off into
the high desert dark with the dogs he loved.
Friends wonder if Kenny settled in some windy
west Texas town with the wild birds.
Or did his heart give out pounding tent poles
in a carnival somewhere?
Perhaps he is staring out at the Salton Sea
where, he told me once,
his throbbing bones might finally be warm.

Locking the Barn

The neighbor's wife has left him.
Morning finds him standing alone
in the wide doorway of his empty barn,
taking long pulls off a hand-rolled cigarette,
watching how clouds have stopped moving.

The sky is dirty gray, air weighted with
the scent of clover and alfalfa.
Mosquitos whine around his head,
so too passages from the Bible he reads
upon waking and before going to sleep.
He thinks he keeps God behind his eyes
but his eyes are also crowded with demons,
the demons who send him stumbling into the night
where he suffers the dark woods of his thoughts.
He reads his holy words for salvation
but the voices are even louder without her,
have spiked tongues, a thorny bitterness
that drives him to strike who he loves.

He locks the barn up tight as a tomb.
Her horses are gone and so is she.
Maybe tomorrow the sun will appear
and the meadow dry out so he can hay,
drive the tractor back and forth, back and forth.

Teenage Boys, Booze and Fast Cars

for damion

The phone rings, opens
the morning like a wound.
"Please see if he's home,"
the detective says.
Car accident.
Oak Tree.
Deceased driver.
Someone else is dead in the car
and they think it is you.

My stomach sinks
like stones in a well,
breath collapses,
plunges down basement stairs.
I call your name at the open door,
you answer
and I tell you who is dead,
lost to you forever.
You are seventeen
and he is your best friend.

Years later on a slight curve of road,
I drive past the place
where the tree once stood.
In the distance the Hadley cornfields
roll away into July sun.
Everything is soft, hot, forgetful.
You are a man now, a police officer,
the one who startles mothers
with early morning phone calls.
A man who never knew how long loss
would sleep inside his heart.

Cowboys and Indians

What is it like to live all these years,
stumbling through vacant fields of loneliness,
every morning the same, same breakfast,
same silence, no one to talk to.
You had not planned for life to turn out this way.
Your parents gone so many years, the dog you
loved dead one morning on the kitchen floor.
When you played cowboys and Indians,
laughter running on your tongue,
did you think sixty would find you lying alone
in a narrow bed in a narrow house.
A bottle of gin under the couch for easy reach,
stacks of scratch tickets on the dusty end table,
mostly two-dollar wins, sometimes forty,
even a thousand dollars once but your pockets
are always empty waiting for the disability check.
The walls of your rooms stained dirty yellow from
cigarette smoke, blinds closed, always dusky inside,
the way you like it. You sit in front of the TV for hours,
rant at Fox News and watch reruns of old westerns.
Outside in the street beneath your windows, traffic waits
at the corner for a light that never seems to change.
You fold laundry and fold the past, put both away in
the moldy closet, the past you take out again and again
like your faded flannel shirts. You remember the
lost girlfriends, fast red car, a cross-country trip
you took forty years ago, the months you lived in exile
hiding from the draft. Sometimes you walk through
city streets at midnight where you move like a refugee
in a torn Navy pea coat, watch-cap pulled down hard
like the past, waiting for something, waiting for
something that never happens.

Daddy's Home
Albuquerque Airport, 2012

I have come home
but I am not the Daddy who left.
I see you now, all three of you
standing next to your mother.
You are waving American flags,
you are holding signs that read
welcome home, daddy.
But I am not the Daddy who left.
I am afraid I am someone else.
Dust at dawn.
The weight of hate.
Blood on my boots.
Dead children that looked just like you,
except you are blond and they were not.
But dead is dead
and I have come home.
I am walking towards you,
through the glass doors
into the room where everyone
waits for someone to come home
or come to love them or come to be.
I will pick you up, embrace you,
but there is a ghost inside me,
a ghost your mother will meet,
a ghost your mother will lie down with
and she will feel the cold pass through her.
She will wonder where I went, who came home.
Scorched orchards.
Boredom and bloated dogs.
Sweat and stink of fear.
Can you smell it all over me
as I pick you up, as I hold you,
wearing my ironed uniform,

my clean hands touching your bright faces?
So I am home.
I am home for the third time.
Who remembers me?

Driving to Little Big Horn

Through Wyoming and Montana
we drive beside creeks…
 Ten Sleep,
     Black Rock,
          Prairie Dog,
               Rosebud,
clear and swift, keeping their stories to themselves.

Horses nod, stand knee-deep in high prairie grass as if time
were hundreds of years ago and white men only slept east of St. Louis.

The sky is blue linen stretched taut and empty to the horizon.

Greasy Grass Creek wanders through flat bottomland.
7,000 Indians camped here once, now the valley rests empty,
a scattering of trees, bloom of wildflowers,
               sleepy horses forgetting.
     On the hill where bones lie buried, meadowlarks flute,
voices sweet, a gurgling warble lifting out of the grasses,
a song heard after the last war cry,
               the long death moaning, an indifferent wind.

Creeks full of memory and singing water,
creeks that felt the mouths of bison, hands of the Lakota…
 Little Goose,
     Dead Horse,
          Lightning,
               Crazy Woman.

V

for Ashley Sims
1990-2012

On the Way to Emerald City

for ashley, sophie and aria

Dorothy and her companions
wandered into a field of poppies,
dreamy and knee deep
in an endless meadow of red flowers.
Hypnotic scent, petals soft,
impossible to deny their seduction.
Lie down, lie down, you are
so exhausted from your travels.
Forget the journey, the destination.
Sleep. Sleep, my pretties.
Be sad no more.
And so Dorothy and Toto,
the Cowardly Lion too,
succumbed to the deadly slumber.
Oblivious. Unconscious. Unafraid.
Not so Tin Man and Scarecrow.
They had no blood coursing through veins,
no flesh to surrender to such sweetness.
But Tin Man and Scarecrow knew fear,
they jumped up and down.
Waved their arms,
floppy straw (*not fire, not fire*)
stiff tin (*oil can, oil can*).
They called on God and the angels,
anyone they could think of,
until at last the Good Witch
drifted down from heaven,
tore open that blue sky
until snow fell
as soft as the red petals,
cold and white,
the scent of poppies gone.
So simple
on the outskirts of Emerald City.

Ashley with Blueberry Eyes

Early evening and the air
swells with the sound of peepers.
A setting sun has flushed the sky
and an early moon is about to rise.

Walking this old dirt road
you have come to find me
as I try to chase the neighbor's
cow back home.
But the black and white heifer,
delighted with her freedom,
has wandered to the far side
of the greening north pasture.
There will be no catching her.

Our granddaughter sees me.
She bounces on your shoulders.
She is a smile.
She is laughter like a song sparrow.

remember this

the trill and bark of frogs
coming up from the farm pond,
horses leaning into the rising dusk
tails swishing
their dreamy eyes watching you
as you close the gate
cross the road
to the barn where muted lights
have been switched on
you are fourteen
finishing chores with your best friend
you smell molasses and dust
leather and lanolin
manure and sweet grass from the
first cut of the south hay field
and before you leave the stable
you hoist your saddle onto the wood rail
hang the halter on a peg
then head home
into the late May evening
to the women who love you

The Three of us at Zuni Pueblo

At All Tribes Trading Post, a Palestinian man
with bulging eyes and a gentle voice,
gifts our granddaughter earrings,
sells us a Corn Maiden necklace.
He has a black dot on his passport,
cannot fly into Tel Aviv without risk of detainment,
is bound to this Pueblo by a pulse of red dust and history,
lifting now in the violent spring winds

       …the dead humming in leafless April trees.

Three Anglo women,
we watch masked and costumed dancers pray for rain,
feet pounding the same kiva ground for centuries,
jangle of ankle bells, drums throbbing,
copper sun setting behind flat rooftops of the plaza.
Our hearts beating in unison.

The Spring She Drove to Georgia

All her bridges were on fire.
No connections remaining
except to the aging women
she loved and sometimes hated.
She was an immigrant trapped
in a geography of failure,
where a forest had
thickened around her,
suffocating and blotting out the sun.

She left behind a room
of smoke and melancholy.
A messy bed her only refuge
where she'd slept hour after hour,
not caring the day passed away.
She suffered a pain that crowded
her heart from the very beginning,
the origins of attachment and exile,
her wandering horses of sorrow.

Grandmothers Weep

They had tried to save her.
Rescued the toddler from
sucking on pizza crust,
fingering the sticky tab on her diaper,
humming in the dark bedroom
where after so many hours alone
she shook the crib to pieces.
Her mother strung on the crack wire.

All those years they loved her, raised her,
but it wasn't enough to heal her abandoned heart
or ease the yawning sorrow that gripped her.

Horse took her sad away,
a drug that seized her by the neck,
shook until she could barely think.
Wandering the kitchen in the dark,
rocking her cat,
her twitching legs not letting her sleep,
all the demons knocking blind behind her eyes.
Upstairs in her room, vomit
in the wastebasket, urine in a cup,
candy wrappers and secrets scattered over the floor,
shades closed, shame hiding in corners
where she waited for a light she couldn't let in.

The grandmothers loved her. They were broken.
They opened the door for her to step out alone.
Nothing more to do but weep.

Track Marks and Sorrow

Snow drives sideways,
a low moan of wind
troubles the window
piling white in a corner
between screen and glass.

I stand by the wood stove,
stare out a different window
at the same snow sweeping
across the south meadow.
I breathe in grief,
the kind that makes you
take to your bed
or drink too much,
the kind that makes you
a ghost...
touch and
your hand
will feel nothing.

She was to be here
for a birthday dinner
instead she lay cold,
dead under a quilt
of blue sorrow.

Early Dark

Light slips away like a life.
The sun moves distant, the earth sighs,
everything shifts, spins while we remain rooted
to an old ground we trust will not move.
But move it does like time, like water, like blood
running through our veins,
endlessly roaming with a
silence we cannot hear even as it
roars in our ears and the light dies
a little more every day.

Did you know when the needle first pierced your skin
that this one time would be one too many
and then never enough?
Did you know a groove was simply waiting to awaken
in your brain, hungry, lonely and insatiable?
Did you understand as you felt the sad slip away
that this was a horse you could not ride,
could not safely lead across any meadow?

How do people live where it is dusk at midday,
where, sightless and dumb, too many of us
wander a polar night, seeking small stones of joy?
The axis of earth tips, a thing we never think about
like worm holes or imploding stars, ice caps melting
and plankton unable to swim against the current.
It is nearly winter.
I place these lines on a piece of paper.
Ashley, can you hear the light now?

Searching for Ashley

At dawn an owl came to my window
with a language of shadow and dream

of grief and light, deep woods where
wind prays high in the trees all day.

Its eyes were soft dark pools,
feather tips illuminated by the rising sun.

Did owl have you tucked under a wing,
wise spirit keeper,

taking your newly freed soul
out of this density to one without sorrow?

Were you humming softly beneath the
swiftly beating heart, the hollow feathers?

Sage, Ruin, Bits of Bone

We wanted to give you something you could not lose
something that would stun you,
tear the sky wide open,
take you in so you could begin again,
this time with your sadness washed away.
But it was not to be, clouds too thick,
sodden with an anguish you could not part with,
an anguish sitting just inside the door to yourself,
a door we could not unlock.

Ruin, rock, sky.

We found ourselves driving on a dirt road
in the middle of nowhere. Grazing land
on either side, nothing but denuded earth,
occasional cattle and skinny horses, relentless
wandering in search of something sustaining.
In the back seat your ashes lay in a soft deerskin pouch,
a photograph of you in my left breast pocket.
Our grief hard and long with the loss of you.
It was your twenty-third birthday and you were dead.

Wind, weeping, bits of bone.

Steep climb up an ancient stairway
to the top of a mesa, parched hike
above a pueblo empty of life for a thousand years.
A harsh wild beauty, but oh how you loved it there,
just a year ago, before you found the cruel horse
you could not stop riding through rivers of blood.
We carried you against our hearts,
made a circle of stones on a shelf of rock.
We gave you to the four directions, to those who
had gone before. We gave you to the wind.

Sage, corn, tobacco, dust.

Burden

for karen

You relieved the tree
its burden of peaches,
its abundance
of small imperfect fruit,
weighing down the limbs
we had propped up
with boards
and an upside down garbage can.
The small tree asked nothing of us,
just grew on a slope of hill,
needing enough water,
hours of sun to ripen fruit.
One at a time you gathered
its offering of sweetness,
unlike your burden of grief,
not relieved by a simple
turn of the stem.
No words can unhook
the sorrow caught in your throat
like something barbed and black.
Grief is a hungry thief
and it has stolen you away.

Baptism

There is a swimming hole in a
crook of the river, deep and cold,
golden-green in sunlight that falls
so quiet from a piece of sky above.
On either bank, leaves of tall trees
shudder in a breeze stirring from the south
and the water against our skin is liquid silk
almost holy in this place along a gray rock ledge.

Last summer you swam here with her
aware of her demons
but innocent of her growing addiction.
She watched you from the edge of the river,
her long legs hanging over the rocks,
smiling at you, secrets sleeping on her tongue.

Today the morning is lovely with summer,
the river warbles over a stretch of stones.
We submerge ourselves in clear cold water
and for just a moment it washes away
the sadness we carry everywhere,
the shock that rattles against our bones.
Rejoice and be glad, I say out loud to the river,
to the soft August air, to you floating near me.

After the Snowfall

Following a bitter icy drizzle
snow fell all day,
swathing each twig and branch,
the north side of every tree trunk.
Our whole hill outlined in white.
Later a full moon rose,
a huge wide eye in a sky of polished dark.
The world took on a luminous quiet.
Come out, I said,
it is lovely beyond belief.
We walked off into the night.
The trees bowed to us.
No sound but our breath,
a lull of words,
the way ahead dreamlike.
A canticle of light and dark.

www.ingramcontent.com/pod-product-compliance
Lightning Source LLC
Chambersburg PA
CBHW020949090426
42736CB00010B/1342